PURCHASING PRODUCTS AT VERY CHEAP WHOLESALE PRICE FROM 1688 USING YOUR SMARTPHONE

1688.com is the largest Chinese based wholesale Marketplace where almost all the sellers on popular ecommerce platforms such as Alibaba, Aliexpress, Gearbest and others buy directly from and resell at up to **4X** the price and it seems that is the cheapest price for that item.

But the problem associated with **1688.com** is that it is a website in Chinese language and meant for people based in China. Yeah, I know you next question would be: **How then can I purchase products from 1688.com since I don't understand Chinese and I am not located in China?**

That is the essence of this guide as it is meant to show you how to go about the entire process.

So follow through the steps below to learn the process involved in purchasing products from 1688.com like a pro:

1. First visit https://www.1688.com website with your smartphone using chrome browser. Chrome browser is recommended for easy language translation. Once the webpage opens on your device, the

page will be automatically be translated to English by chrome browser as seen in the screenshot below.

2. After the page has been translated to English, type the name of the product you want to purchase into the search box. I'll use 'Photocatalyst Mosquito Killer Lamp' as the product for this illustration. Notice in the screenshot below that my search term 'photocatalyst mosquito killer lamp' did not display any product in the search result. This is because 1688.com is a Chinese website and most of the sellers use Chinese Language to list their products. So if your product search did not yield any result, don't worry, I'll show you a way around it.

3. If your search displayed a page similar to the above screenshot, showing 0 search result, there are a few tricks that can be used to find your product. They are as follows:

  a. Use a different word combination to get a name match with products listed on the site. (**this method will take a lot of time**)

  b. Translate the product name to Chinese using Google translate and then search for the Chinese translation instead. (***This is the best option and the one we'll be using***).

So continue with the next step to translate your product name to Chinese.

4. Visit Google translate page on **https://translate.google.com** via a new browser tab and type the product name in the provided text box, which will show above it on the left that the detected language is English. Make sure the translated language is set to Chinese (simplified) on the right side as shown in the screen below.

5. Copy the Chinese translation of the product name from Google translate page. See the above screenshot.

6. Go back to 1688.com page and paste the copied product name translation in the search box; you should now see matching products displayed on the search result page.

7. Scroll through the products, taking note of their **prices** and **number of transaction.** Using the 'photocatalyst mosquito killer lamp' in my case, I found one with very low price and a good number of transactions. See the screenshot below.

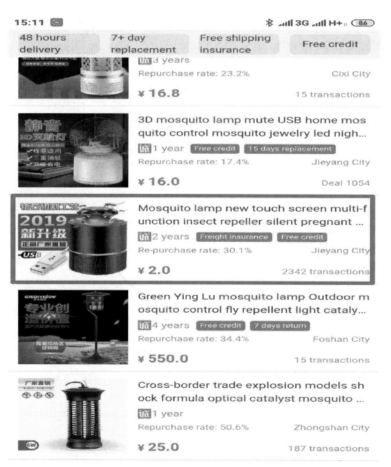

8. Click on the product to display its full description page. Here also take note of the number of positive feedbacks and rating of the

product. Only consider products with at least 10 total feedbacks/reviews and a minimum rating of 4.0 stars. In this case, the 'photocatalyst mosquito killer lamp' I selected has 203 reviews, most of which are positive and a rating of 4.7 stars as seen below.

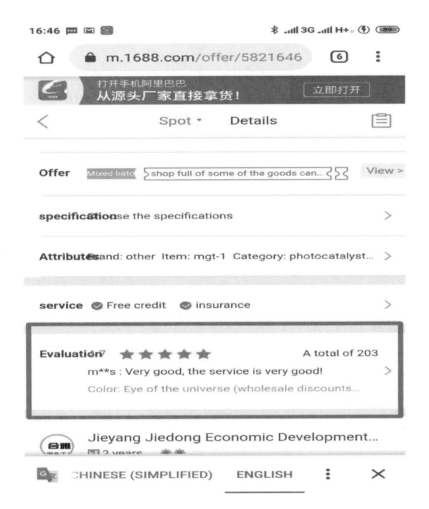

Click on the evaluation to read some of the reviews in order to be sure of what others are saying about the product. Also scroll down to view the full product description in order not to miss some useful information such as manufacturer's contact details etc.

9. Take note of the price to be sure. In this example, the price of the photocatalyst mosquito killer lamp is between ¥1.9 - ¥19.6 as seen in the screenshot below (currency is Chinese Yuan or RMB). This is equivalent to $0.27 - $2.7 per item.

Note: Most times, the price of the product will vary with the quantity, the more quantity you buy, the lesser the price. The screenshot above shows a price range of 1.96 to 19.6 Yuan i.e. if you purchase a very large quantity, you can get the product at a unit price of 1.96 Yuan. Sometimes the prices for each corresponding quantity will be listed, so take note of that.

10.   Once you are satisfied with your evaluation of the product. It is time to make all necessary arrangements to purchase it.

11.   While on the product description page. Click on the button with text **'Entering the shop'** located just below the Evaluation section. This will take you to the merchants shop page.

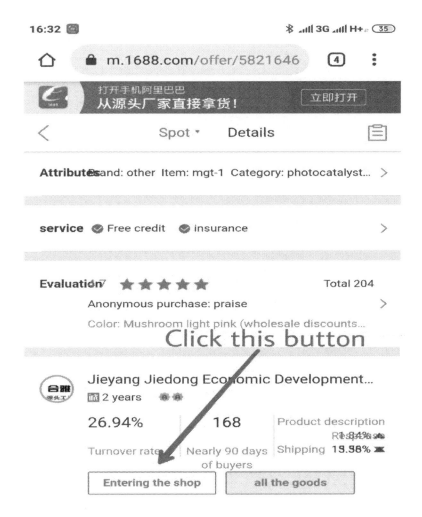

12.   On the shop page, at the bottom of your smartphone screen, you should see a navigation link among others titled 'Company Profile'. Click on this link to go to the company's information page.

Note: While navigating from one page to another, chrome browser will automatically translate the texts on the current page from Chinese to English. If yours doesn't automatically translate the pages as you navigate, first refresh the page, if that doesn't work, then check the chrome browser app settings on your smartphone.

13.   On the company's profile page, click on the orange button with text **'dial number'** fixed to the bottom of the screen as seen in *screenshot 1* below. If you don't see the dial number button, it means the Google translate bar which is sometimes visible at the bottom of your screen is directly on top of the button making it invisible. Just click on the **X** to close the Google translate bar to make the orange dial number button visible. See *screenshot 2* below.

Screenshot 1

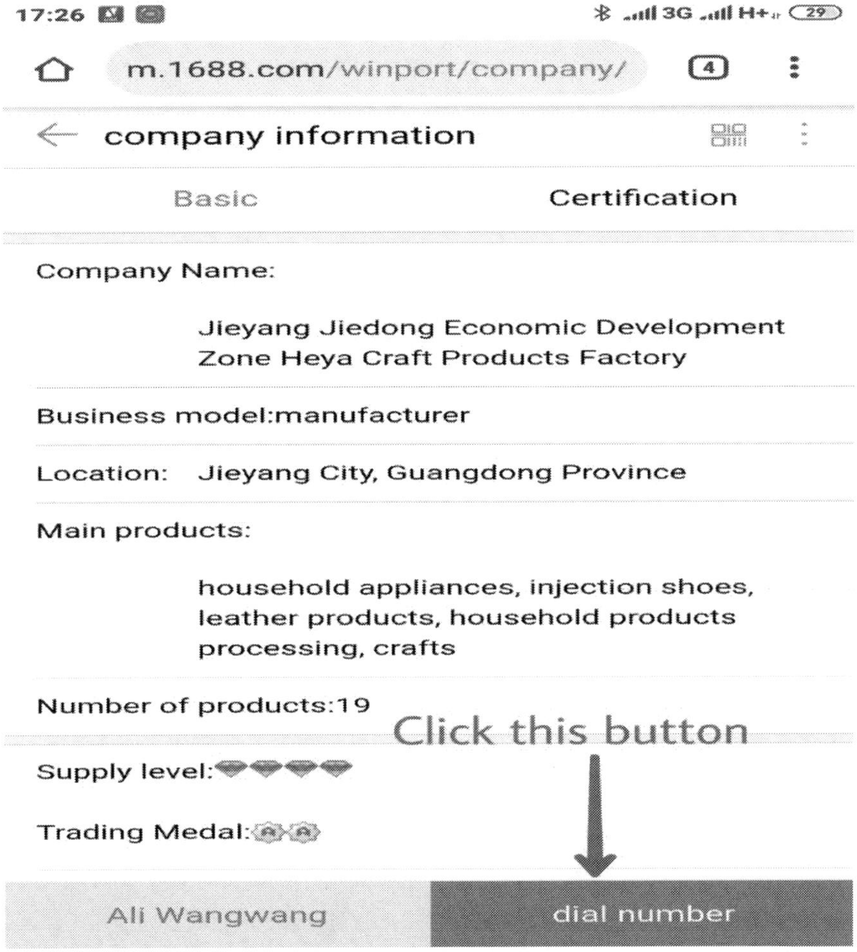

🏠   m.1688.com/winport/company/   4   ⋮

←   company information   ▫▫   ⋮

Basic   Certification

Company Name:

Jieyang Jiedong Economic Development
Zone Heya Craft Products Factory

Business model:manufacturer

Location: Jieyang City, Guangdong Province

Main products:

household appliances, injection shoes,
leather products, household products
processing, crafts

Number of products:19

Click this button

Supply level:♦♦♦♦

Trading Medal:⟨Ⓐ⟩⟨Ⓐ⟩

| Ali Wangwang | dial number |

Screenshot 2

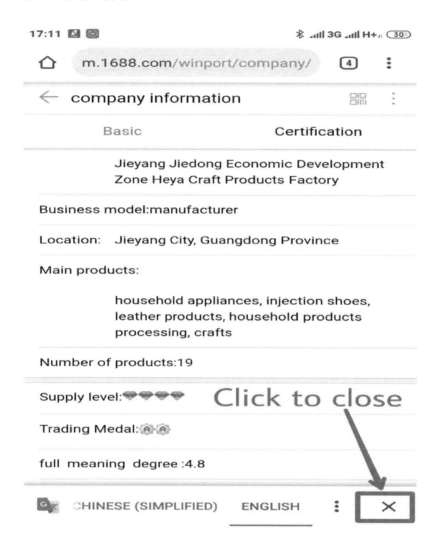

14.　Clicking the orange dial number button should display a phone number as seen in the screenshot below. Click on the phone number that displays to automatically copy it to the phone dialer screen.

← company information

Basic   Certification

Company Name:

Jieyang Jiedong Economic Development
Zone Heya Craft Products Factory

Business model:manufacturer

Location: Jieyang City, Guangdong Province

Main products:

household appliances, injection shoes,
leather products, household products
processing, crafts

Number of products:19

Supply level:

18666323010

cancel

Note: if for some reason a phone number does not display when you click on the orange dial number button, then check the product description page for the company's contact information which is sometimes included there also as seen in the screenshot below.

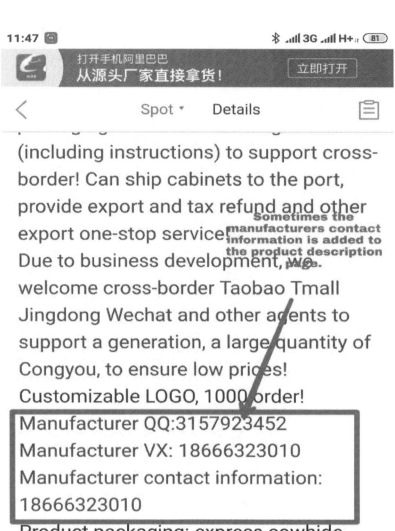

Content visible in screenshot:

11:47

Spot ▾   Details

(including instructions) to support cross-border! Can ship cabinets to the port, provide export and tax refund and other export one-stop service! Due to business development, we welcome cross-border Taobao Tmall Jingdong Wechat and other agents to support a generation, a large quantity of Congyou, to ensure low prices! Customizable LOGO, 1000 order!

Manufacturer QQ:3157923452
Manufacturer VX: 18666323010
Manufacturer contact information: 18666323010

Product packaging: express cowhide box (13cm*13cm*19.5cm), gross weight: 380g

Sometimes the manufacturers contact information is added to the product description page.

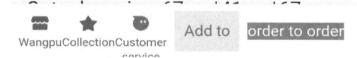

WangpuCollectionCustomer service   Add to   order to order

15.   On the phone dialer screen, add +86 in front of the displayed number. This is the Chinese country code and now the number should look like the screenshot below.

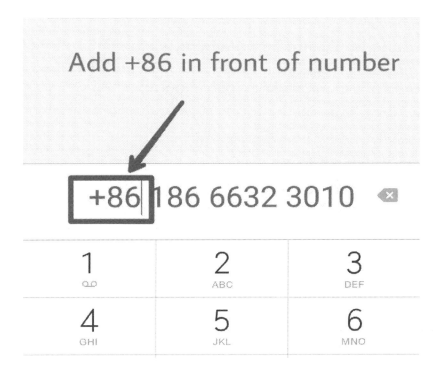

16.	Proceed to save the phone number with a name that can be easily remembered e.g. 'mosquito killer lamp' or whatever is the name of your product. You'll need this phone number to contact the seller/manufacturer which is another process altogether.

Congratulations, you are one step away from contacting the manufacturer. This ends phase 1 of sourcing the products yourself like a pro. Next I will take you through the process of communicating with the manufacturer to negotiate and arrange for the purchase of your product.

CONTACTING THE PRODUCT MANUFACTURER/SELLER

Before you contact the seller, you'll need to have the following apps installed on your smartphone: **WhatsApp and WeChat.**

After installing the above mentioned apps, follow the steps below to contact the product seller. By now you should already have the contact phone number of the product seller stored in your phone.

1. First find out if the seller uses WhatsApp messaging platform for communication by searching for their phone number using your installed WhatsApp app. Although, there is a very little chance that the seller will be found on WhatsApp, because 95% of them only communicate via **WeChat** which is one of the world's biggest Chinese multipurpose messaging, social media and mobile payment app. So if you don't find the seller on WhatsApp, you'll likely find them on WeChat. So proceed to the next step.

2. Open WeChat app on your smartphone. On the chat screen, click on the **+** sign located at the top right corner to bring up a menu.

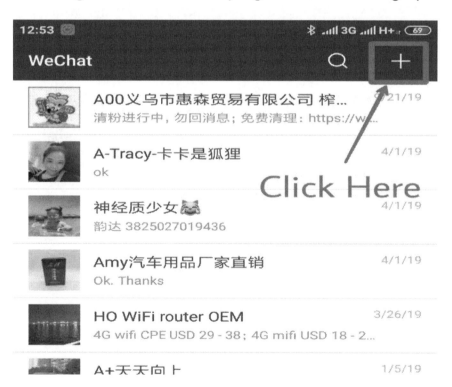

3. Next, click the ' **Add Contacts** ' option on the menu that appears as seen in the screenshot below.

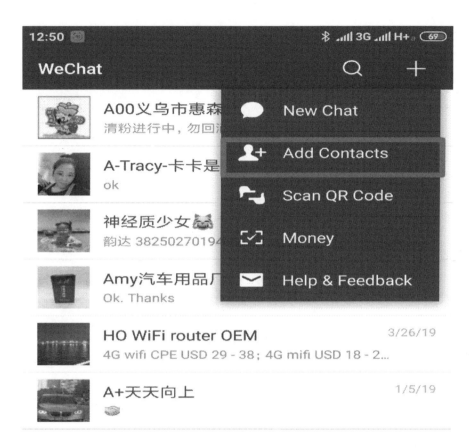

4. On the Add Contacts page, click on the **'Mobile Contacts'** option. This will enable you to add a contact saved in your phonebook. See screenshot below.

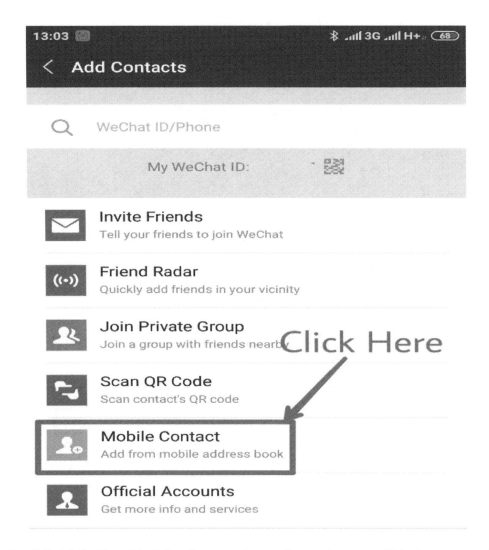

5. Clicking the Mobile Contacts option above will bring up a list of all your contacts that are registered on the WeChat Platform. Scroll to find the product manufacturer's number you saved previously.

6. Next, click on the **Add** button at the right side of the name to add the contact to your friends list as seen in the screenshot below.

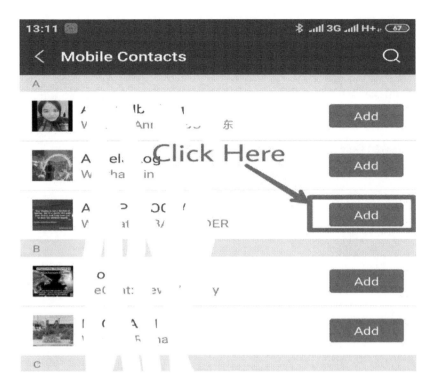

7. You'll be taken to the next screen which will ask you to first send a friend request to the contact. You'll also need to type a short message before sending the friend request such as. **'Hi, I am interested in your product......'** in order for the seller to know you are contacting them for business purpose.

8. Next click the **send** button located at the top right corner of your screen after typing the message to send the friend request as seen in the screenshot below.

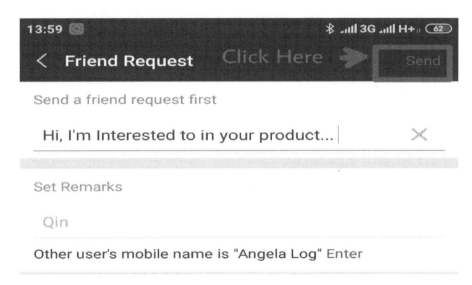

9. It may take up to 24 hours before you get a response. Once they have accepted your request, you'll first get this message **"I've accepted your friend request. Now let's chat!"** as an automated response from the seller to indicate that they have accepted your friend request. See screenshot below.

Also notice from the above screenshot that the seller replied with a message in Chinese language after the above automated message. One great feature of the WeChat app is its ability to automatically translate Chinese words to English... So for example if you get a reply from your seller in Chinese, you can simply **long press** on the Chinese text to bring up an option to translate it into English as seen in screenshot below.

The Chinese word translates to '**Hello**' in English as seen in the screenshot below.

10. Continue the conversation with the seller about your interest in purchasing the product.

See screenshots below of the conversation I had with the seller of the 'Photocatalyst Mosquito killer Lamp' after their response to my friends request below **(please read the conversation from the screenshots from top to bottom in order to understand).**

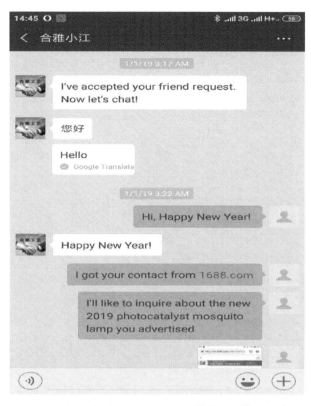

合雅小江

I've accepted your friend request. Now let's chat!

您好

Hello
Google Translate

1/1/19 3:22 AM

Hi, Happy New Year!

Happy New Year!

I got your contact from 1688.com

I'll like to inquire about the new 2019 photocatalyst mosquito lamp you advertised

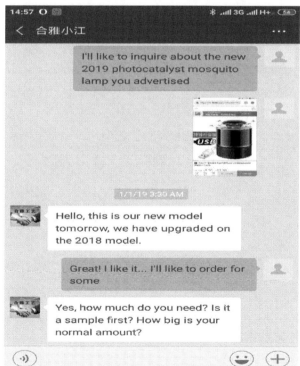

合雅小江

I'll like to inquire about the new 2019 photocatalyst mosquito lamp you advertised

1/1/19 3:30 AM

Hello, this is our new model tomorrow, we have upgraded on the 2018 model.

Great! I like it... I'll like to order for some

Yes, how much do you need? Is it a sample first? How big is your normal amount?

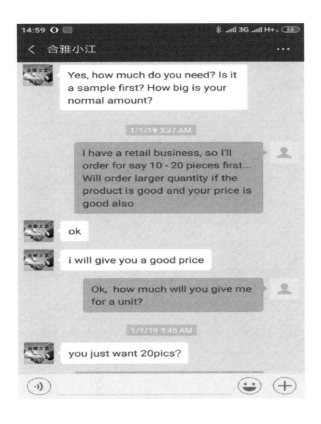

Yes, how much do you need? Is it a sample first? How big is your normal amount?

1/1/19 3:37 AM

I have a retail business, so I'll order for say 10 - 20 pieces first... Will order larger quantity if the product is good and your price is good also

ok

i will give you a good price

Ok, how much will you give me for a unit?

1/1/19 3:45 AM

you just want 20pics?

you just want 20pics?

Yes I'll get about that quantity for a start

1/1/19 4:18 AM

i see

1/1/19 4:30 AM

the price is 15.9 for one pic

¥15.9

1/1/19 5:38 AM

Ok. Please can I see real images and a video of the product if possible

1/1/19 9:00 AM

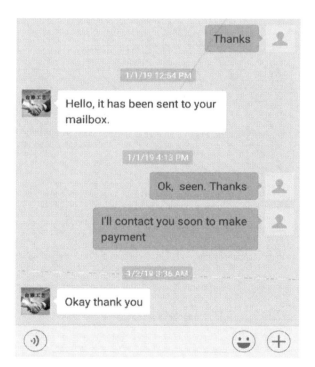

Me: Hi, Happy New Year!

Seller: Happy New Year!

Me: I got your contact from 1688.com

Me: I'll like to inquire about the new 2019 photocatalyst mosquito lamp you advertised

Seller: Hello, this is our new model tomorrow, we have upgraded on the 2018 model.

Me: Great! I like it... I'll like to order for some

Seller: Yes, how much do you need? Is it a sample first? How big is your normal amount?

Me: I have a retail business, so I'll order for say 10 - 20 pieces first... Will order larger quantity if the product is good and your price is good also.

Seller: ok

Seller: i will give you a good price

Me: Ok, how much will you give me for a unit?

Seller: you just want 20pics ?

Me: Yes I'll get about that quantity for a start

Seller: i see

Seller: the price is 15.9 for one pic

Seller: ¥15.9 (i.e approx $2.22)

Me: Ok. Please can I see real images and a video of the product if possible

Seller: Ok

Seller: (Attached a Video file)

Me: Hi, please I can't view the video. Can you send to me via email: ca******@gmail.com

Me: Thanks.

Seller: Hello, it has been sent to your mailbox.

Me: Ok, seen. Thanks

Me: I'll contact you soon to make payment

Seller: Okay thank you.

So you can see how the conversation with the seller went and ended with my reply of getting back to make payment. You can use this conversation as a guide when communicating with sellers.

11.   The next thing to do after agreeing with the seller about the price is to make the necessary arrangements for the product purchase.

PAYING FOR YOUR GOODS

There are various ways to pay for your goods; I'll talk about the 3 best and effective ways available. They are:

1. Paying in dollars through PayPal
2. Paying in Yuan through your freight forwarder.
3. Using online exchangers / third party services to pay for your goods.

I'll further explain these methods below:

1. Paying in Dollars through PayPal

PayPal is a universal and popular payment channel used by merchants worldwide, for this reason, some of the sellers on 1688.com will accept payment for your ordered goods via PayPal which makes it easier for you to quickly pay and ship your order.

2. Payment In RMB Through Your Freight Forwarder

Most times sellers on 1688.com only accept payment in their local Chinese currency which is Yuan or RMB, since you do not have a means to pay in Yuan, a way out of this is to have your freight forwarding/shipping agent make the payment on your behalf.

The seller will provide their Account details (Alipay or Bank Account number) which you will send to your freight forwarder via WhatsApp for them to make the payment on your behalf. Your freight forwarder will ask you to pay the equivalent into their PayPal or bank account at the given exchange rate after which they'll proceed to make the payment on your behalf. Remember your goods will also be sent to the freight forwarding company's address after payment.

3. Using Online Exchangers/Third Party Services To Pay For Your Goods

You may not have an available means of making payment either through PayPal or your freight forwarder and may urgently need to pay your seller.

This is where the online exchangers/payment services come in. This individuals or businesses provide foreign exchange and payment services for people online, they can help you pay the seller for your goods at a small fee. All you have to do is send them the seller's account details such as PayPal email address, Alipay or Bank Account. They will then make the transfer and give you a screenshot of the transaction which you will send to the seller as proof of your payment. (see the resource section for contacts of trusted online foreign exchangers.)

After the seller has confirmed the receipt of your payment, they will proceed to send your goods to your freight forwarder who will then arrange the goods for shipping to your location.

SHIPPING YOUR GOODS

There are various methods available for shipping your ordered goods to your location.

They are as follows:

1. Air mail / Post (Avoid using this)
2. Expedited Shipping such as DHL, EMS, UPS etc. (Avoid this)
3. Using a Freight Forwarding / Shipping Company (Best option)

1. Shipping via Air Mail / Postal Services

The seller will ship your goods via air mail / post. Although this method is cheap but it is highly not recommended because it can take a very long time approximately 30 - 45 business days or more for your goods to get to your nearest post office. If you are lucky, the goods can get to you in 2 - 3 weeks. Moreover, it is not a secure shipping method as the goods may get lost in transit, damaged or tampered with. So by all means, avoid using this method.

2. Using Expedited Shipping

The seller will ship your goods using very fast shipping companies such as DHL, UPS, EMS etc. It'll only take approximately 3 - 5 business days for your goods to get to your location but these methods are highly expensive and not recommended for Mini Importation Business if you are out to make good profit. Remember that the heavier your goods is, the more money you'll pay for shipping. So avoid using expedited shipping methods for your goods.

3. Using A Freight Forwarding Company (Best option)

This is the best and recommended shipping option suitable for the Mini Importation. Using this method, the seller will send your goods to the freight forwarding / shipping company's address located in China that you'll send to them.

Steps

1. First you'll need to find a good freight forwarding company that will handle the shipping of your products from China to your location. See resource section (last section) for some freight forwarding companies.

2. Once you have contacted the freight forwarder, they will send you their shipping address with any other instruction which you will need to send to the seller.

3. Proceed to send the shipping address to the seller via your channel of communication i.e. WeChat with the instruction that they should include your full name, address, phone number and tracking number on the package before sending it to your freight forwarder.

4. Don't also forget to ask the seller to send you the tracking number of the package(s) that you want delivered to the freight forwarding company's address. This information is needed as it'll be used to identify your package once it arrives at the freight forwarding company's address since they get a lot of packages from different individuals and businesses also. Please don't forget this.

5. After the seller has sent you the tracking number of the goods which will be delivered to your freight forwarding company address, you should send the tracking number to your freight forwarder, so that they can identify the package as yours once it arrives.

7. Your freight forwarder will contact you immediately your package arrives, this will take only a few days, sometimes within 24 hours depending on distance between the seller's location and freight forwarder's location.

Note: Sometimes you may have ordered different products from different sellers who will send the respective products to the freight forwarding company at different times, please take note of the tracking number of each package and send same to your freight forwarder who will acknowledge collection of the packages as they are delivered.

8. Once your freight forwarder has contacted you about the arrival of your goods, the next step is to arrange for shipping of the goods to your location which will be handled by the freight forwarding company.

That's All! You may have to wait for a couple of days (less than a week or two) to receive your purchased items down to your location.

RESOURCES

Freight Forwarding Companies/Agents:

You can simply do a Google search of freight forwarding companies based on your location e.g freight forwarding company China to USA.

Some International Freight Forwarders in China.

1. www.rayssun.com

Conact Person: claire@rayssun.com

whatapp: +8618122153331

2. nicolehuang@cn.evergreen-logistics.com

3. Ask the sellers, they can direct you to a good freight forwarding company in China.

Contact ctec25services@gmail.com for support.

PAYMENT

If you need help to pay of sellers via PayPal or RMB, Contact ctec25services@gmail.com

Made in the USA
Columbia, SC
18 October 2020